Prologue

"The Roof That Could Save the World (and Your Bottom Line)"

Congratulations!

You've just picked up the most riveting book ever written about... rooftops.

Yes, rooftops...

But not just any rooftops—your rooftop. The one you barely think about unless it's leaking, covered in snow, or playing host to a flock of very noisy pigeons.

Here's the thing: your rooftop is a superstar in disguise. It's a 9-to-5 slacker when it could be a 24/7 MVP. It's time to flip the script and turn that underutilised space into a lean, green, money-saving machine.

How, you ask?

With solar panels. Yes, those shiny, futuristic tiles that make you feel like you're living in a sci-fi movie. Except this isn't fiction. This is your business's reality - and an opportunity so bright, you'll need sunglasses.

If you're reading this, chances are you've either:

Contact me:

- Heard your competitors are installing solar panels and felt a pang of FOMO
- Got hit with your last energy bill and wondered if you're secretly funding a private jet for your utility provider.

Whatever brought you here, welcome…

This book is your friendly, slightly sarcastic guide to the endless benefits of going solar.

It's specifically tailored for manufacturing and engineering companies because, let's face it, you guys use *a lot* of electricity.

But instead of viewing your power needs as a problem, why not see them as an opportunity?

With solar panels, every kilowatt-hour is a chance to save money, save the planet, and save yourself from the headaches of unpredictable energy costs.

Oh, and don't worry - this isn't one of those dry, technical manuals full of jargon and charts you'll pretend to read during meetings.

We're going to keep it simple, a little funny, and refreshingly honest.

Think of this book as the solar panel consultant who tells you the truth without trying to upsell you a backup battery the size of a minivan.

Contact me:

By the time you finish, you'll not only understand why your empty rooftop is the biggest missed opportunity since someone rejected the Beatles, but you'll also be itching to call a solar installer. And if you don't, well, at least you'll have some great facts to casually drop at the next company barbecue.

So, grab a coffee, find a sunny spot to read (how fitting!), and let's dive into the surprisingly exciting world of solar power for your business.

By the end, your roof will never look the same again. And neither will your electric bill.

Let's get started, shall we?

Table of Contents:

Chapter 1 – How Solar Energy Works: Harnessing the Sun's Free Lunch **Page 5**

Chapter 2 – Why Solar Loves Big Roofs (And It Cannot Lie) **Page 12**

Chapter 3 – Why Solar Panels and Big Roofs Are a Match Made in Heaven **Page 20**

Chapter 4 – 5 Signs You Have the Perfect Roof for Solar Panels **Page 29**

Chapter 5 – Electricity Bills: The Villain of Your Balance Sheet **Page 36**

Chapter 6 – Solar ROI, Asset Finance, and Free-to-Fit: Saving Money (and the Planet) One Slice at a Time **Page 45**

Chapter 7 – Solar Myths Busted: The Truth About Panels, Roofs, and the Weather **Page 53**

Chapter 8 – Going Solar: The Ultimate Green Glow-Up for Your Business **Page 61**

Chapter 9 – Smiling CFOs and Sunny Profits: How Energy Savings Brighten the Bottom-Line **Page 69**

Chapter 10 – "Solar Power - No, It Won't Fry Your Toaster". **Page 77**

Chapter 11 – "The Sunny Side of Saving - A Conclusion That's Worth Its Weight in Watts" **Page 85**

Chapter 12 – About the Author **Page 92**

Contact me:

Chapter 1: How Solar Energy Works: Harnessing the Sun's Free Lunch

Welcome to Solar 101

Let's start with the basics: solar energy comes from the sun.

That giant glowing ball of gas in the sky?

It's been blasting out free energy for about 4.6 billion years.

In fact, every hour, the sun delivers enough energy to Earth to power the entire planet for a year. And yet, most of us are still paying through the nose for electricity.

Why? Because we've been too busy staring at screens instead of rooftops.

But don't worry - you're about to join the enlightened.

Let's break it down step by step so you'll understand why solar energy, isn't just science; it's a cosmic life hack.

Step 1: The Sun Does All the Heavy Lifting

Imagine the sun as the ultimate overachiever. It's a 24/7 nuclear fusion reactor sitting 93 million miles away, sending energy to Earth in the form of light and heat. It doesn't ask for a salary, vacation days, or even a thank-you card. And yet, here it is, throwing free energy at us day after day.

Step 2: Photons: The Energy Delivery Guys

The sun sends energy to Earth in the form of photons.

Think of photons as tiny packets of sunlight.

They're like those delivery drivers who bring your packages - except photons don't get stuck in traffic or leave your stuff on the neighbours' patio.

When photons hit a solar panel, they bring their energy with them. This is where the magic starts to happen.

Step 3: Solar Panels: The Great Energy Catchers

Solar panels are the sun's version of flypaper.

They're made of special materials - usually silicon - that love catching photons.

Each solar panel is like a giant energy sponge, soaking up sunlight and converting it into electricity. But how does that work, exactly?

Picture this...

When photons hit the silicon in a solar panel, they get the electrons inside all excited. And when electrons are excited, they start moving around like kids in a bouncy house. This movement of electrons is what creates electricity. It's called the **photovoltaic effect**, but we'll just call it "science sorcery" for now.

Step 4: The Electric Current: Energy on the Move

Now that the electrons are all hyped up, they need somewhere to go. Enter the electric circuit.

Solar panels are designed with built-in wiring that guides these excited electrons into a current.

Think of it like organising a group of rowdy kids into a conga line. Once the electrons start moving in the right direction, *bam*! You've got electricity.

But wait - it's not quite ready to use yet.

That's because the electricity coming out of solar panels is in direct current (DC) form.

Most of the stuff you use (like your toaster, laptop, or industrial machinery) runs on alternating current (AC).

Don't worry; we've got a gadget for that.

Step 5: Meet the Inverter: The Translator of Electricity

Think of the inverter as the Rosetta Stone for energy.

It takes the DC electricity from your solar panels and converts it into AC electricity that your appliances and machines can understand.

Without the inverter, your solar setup would be about as useful as a smartphone without a charger.

The inverter is where the raw power of the sun gets refined into something you can plug into. It's like taking raw cocoa beans and turning them into chocolate. Delicious, usable, electric chocolate.

Step 6: Powering Your Business: The Endgame

Once the inverter has done its job, the electricity flows into your building's power system, ready to light up your factory floor, spin your machines, or keep your coffee machine buzzing.

And the best part?

Any excess energy your solar panels produce can be sent back to the grid or stored in a battery for later use.

It's like having a backup plan for your backup plan.

Why Solar Energy Works Everywhere

You might be thinking…

"But what about cloudy days? Or places where the sun doesn't shine 24/7?"

Great questions! Here's the deal:

Solar panels work even when it's cloudy - sure, they're not at full capacity, but they still generate power from indirect sunlight.

Energy storage has your back - with modern battery systems, you can store the electricity your solar panels generate during the day and use it at night or on rainy days. It's like saving leftovers for later.

So, unless you're operating in a pitch-black cave (and if you are, let's talk about life choices), solar energy can work for you.

Common Misconceptions About Solar Energy

"Do solar panels suck energy from the sun?"

Nope.

The sun is so powerful that we could cover the entire Earth with solar panels, and it wouldn't even notice. It's like taking one grain of rice out of a Costco-sized bag.

"Will solar panels work in winter?"

Absolutely!

Solar panels care about light, not heat. They're like cats - perfectly happy as long as the sun is shining.

"Aren't solar panels only for hippies?"

Not anymore!

Today's solar panels are sleek, modern, and ready to rock your industrial rooftop. They're like the leather jackets of energy solutions: cool and functional.

Fun Facts About Solar Energy

- Solar power is so abundant that in one second, the sun produces enough energy to meet global demand for 500,000 years. (Yes, you read that right.)
- The International Space Station runs entirely on solar power, proving that if it works in space, it can definitely handle your factory in Sheffield.
- Solar panels have no moving parts, meaning they're silent, low-maintenance, and unlikely to call in sick.

Contact me:

Why It's Time to Go Solar

To sum it up, solar energy is simple, effective, and endlessly entertaining once you realise, you're harnessing the power of a literal star.

It's clean, it's renewable, and it's the ultimate power move for any manufacturing or engineering company that wants to slash electricity costs.

So, the next time you see the sun – remember - it's not just a pretty face. It's your ticket to lower bills, higher profits, and a greener future.

What are you waiting for?

Let the sun do the heavy lifting - it's been waiting 4.6 billion years for this.

Contact me:

Chapter 2: Why Solar Loves Big Roofs (And It Cannot Lie)

Let's Talk Roofs

If you're running a manufacturing or engineering company, chances are you've got a sprawling rooftop that's been silently sitting there, doing a whole lot of nothing.

Sure, it's been protecting your precious machinery from rain, birds, and the occasional drone gone rogue.

But beyond that, what has your roof *really* done for you lately?

Here's the thing…

That vast expanse of roof is practically begging to make itself useful. And solar panels are the perfect tenants - quiet, hardworking, and always paying their rent in electricity savings.

Let's dive into why your big, underutilised rooftop is a solar goldmine.

1. Big Roofs, Big Potential

Think of your rooftop as prime real estate. Every square meter up there represents an opportunity to capture sunlight and turn it into savings.

The bigger the roof, the more panels you can install. The more panels you install, the more energy you generate. And the more energy you generate, the more you save.

It's like playing Tetris but with sunlight - and the only thing you're stacking is profit.

Here's a fun fact…

A typical industrial solar panel can generate about 300 watts of power.

With just 1,000 square meters of rooftop space, you could install roughly 600 panels, producing enough electricity to power dozens of homes - or, more importantly, your energy-hungry operations.

2. A Roof That Works Overtime

Your roof is already working full-time protecting your building.

But why stop there?

Solar panels let your roof pull double duty. While it keeps the weather out, the panels soak up sunlight and convert it into electricity for your business.

And the best part?

Solar panels don't need lunch breaks, health insurance, or overtime pay.

They just sit there, soaking up the sun, and generating energy like the reliable overachievers they are.

3. Energy Where You Need It

One of the biggest advantages of installing solar panels on your roof is that the energy they generate is used right where it's produced.

No need for long-distance power transmission that wastes energy along the way.

Your rooftop generates the electricity, and your machines, lights, and coffee machines use it.

It's the shortest supply chain you'll ever see - and it's 100% efficient.

4. Free Real Estate, No Rent to Pay

Here's the beauty of your roof…

Contact me:

It's already paid for. No monthly rent, no mortgage.

It's just sitting there, waiting for you to turn it into an asset.

Installing solar panels doesn't require you to buy more land or build new infrastructure. You're simply making better use of what you already have.

Think of it like finding a forgotten £50 note in your jacket pocket - except this £50 - keeps giving back for the next 25 years.

5. Perfect for Large-Scale Energy Needs

If your business consumes a lot of electricity, a large rooftop solar system is a no-brainer.

Industrial operations often run machines, lights, HVAC systems, and more - all of which gulp down electricity faster than a dehydrated camel.

With a rooftop solar setup, you can offset a significant portion of your electricity use.

For example…

A manufacturing facility spending £20,000 a month on electricity could easily reduce its energy costs by 50% or more with the right solar installation.

That's like giving yourself an annual raise of £120,000 - and who doesn't love a raise?

6. Solar Panels Are Low-Maintenance Workhorses

Let's address a common worry...

"But won't I have to spend a fortune maintaining all those panels?"

Absolutely not.

Solar panels are practically the golden retrievers of technology - reliable, low-maintenance, and always ready to work.

Once installed, they require very little attention.

A simple annual cleaning and inspection are usually enough to keep them in top shape. They have no moving parts, so there's nothing to wear out or break down. They just sit there, silently working for you, year after year.

7. Climate Control for Your Building

Here's a bonus perk...

Solar panels can help regulate the temperature inside your building.

By covering your roof, they act as a barrier that reduces heat absorption during the summer. This means your building stays cooler, and you spend less on air-conditioning.

Think of it as giving your roof a stylish pair of sunglasses - it's functional and fabulous.

8. The Green Factor: Marketing Gold

In today's world, being eco-friendly isn't just good for the planet - it's good for business.

Customers, partners, and investors love companies that take sustainability seriously.

By installing solar panels, you're making a bold statement: "We care about the environment, and we're doing something about it."

Your rooftop solar system isn't just an energy solution; it's a giant green billboard.

Every client or customer who visits your facility will see those gleaming panels and know you are part of the solution, not the problem.

9. Government Incentives and Perks

Installing solar panels isn't just good for your bottom line - it's often subsidised by the government.

Depending on where you're located, you might qualify for tax breaks, grants, or feed-in tariffs.

For example, in the UK...

- The Smart Export Guarantee (SEG) allows you to sell excess electricity back to the grid.
- The government allow you to write off the full installation cost against company profits - saving you the corporation tax - making the return on investment much quicker.

It's like the government saying, "Thanks for helping the planet. Here's some extra cash."

10. Futureproofing Your Business

Energy prices are unpredictable, but one thing's for sure - they're not going down anytime soon.

By investing in solar, you're locking in lower energy costs for the next 25 years or more.

It's like buying a lifetime supply of coffee at today's prices - except instead of caffeine, you're getting clean energy.

And with every energy price hike, you'll feel like a genius for making the switch.

The Takeaway

Your roof has been patiently waiting for its moment in the spotlight.

By installing solar panels, you're not just reducing your electricity bills - you're transforming an underutilised asset into a money-saving, planet-saving powerhouse.

So, take a look at your rooftop. Imagine it covered in sleek, shiny solar panels, soaking up the sun and working tirelessly to power your business. It's time to let your roof live up to its full potential.

And remember…

The bigger the roof, the bigger the savings.

If your roof is the size of a football pitch, congratulations - you're about to score big in the game of solar.

Chapter 3: Why Solar Panels and Big Roofs Are a Match Made in Heaven

Let's Face It: Your Roof Isn't Pulling Its Weight

Take a moment to think about your company's rooftop.

What's it doing right now?

Probably just sitting there, collecting rainwater, bird droppings, and the occasional wayward frisbee.

But what if I told you that your roof could transform from a lazy loafer into a hardworking, money-making superhero? Enter: solar panels.

Your sprawling, underutilised rooftop is like an empty plot of land in Monopoly - full of potential, but currently doing squat for your bottom line.

Let's change that - solar panels are the perfect tenants for your roof.

They don't throw loud parties, they don't demand maintenance, and they don't argue about parking spaces. All they do is make you money.

Here are the top reasons why your big, lonely roof is practically begging for a solar makeover - and why you'll laugh all the way to the bank.

1. Your Roof Is a Sunbather Who Needs a Job

Your roof spends all day lying in the sun like it's on a perpetual holiday in Ibiza.

Sure, it's doing an okay job of keeping the rain out and the pigeons away, but honestly - it could be doing so much more.

Solar panels are like the ultimate multitaskers.

They soak up all that sunshine and convert it into electricity, effectively turning your sun-loving roof into a productive employee.

Think of it this way: why let your roof sit idle when it could be working 9-to-5, generating clean energy and slashing your electricity bills?

It's like putting your couch potato nephew to work in the family business - only with far better results.

2. Solar Panels Make Your Roof Look Smarter

Let's be honest: industrial rooftops aren't exactly architectural masterpieces.

They're flat, grey, and boring.

But slap some shiny solar panels up there, and suddenly your building looks like the headquarters of a cutting-edge tech company.

Passersby will think you're on the forefront of innovation, even if you're just producing widgets or custom sprockets.

In short, solar panels don't just save money - they make you look good doing it. It's like putting a suit on your building and giving it a promotion.

3. Big Roof? Big Energy Potential

The size of your roof matters - especially when it comes to solar.

The bigger the roof, the more panels you can install. The more panels you install, the more electricity you generate.

It's basic maths, but with a lot more sunshine involved.

Here's a quick calculation:

- A single industrial solar panel produces about 300 watts of electricity.
- If your roof is large enough to hold 1,000 panels, that's 300 kilowatts of power generated every hour the sun's shining.

- Over a year, that adds up to enough electricity to power an entire small town - or, more importantly, your entire operation.

It's like turning your roof into an energy factory that works 24/7 (or at least during daylight hours).

4. You Already Own or Rent the Real Estate

Here's a fun fact…

Your roof is *free*. Well, sort of.

You've already paid for it, and now it's just sitting there, waiting to be put to work.

Unlike other investments, solar panels don't require you to buy more land or build new structures.

You're simply making better use of what you already have.

It's like discovering a hidden storage space in your house and turning it into a money-making Airbnb. Except instead of tourists, you're hosting sunlight.

5. Solar Panels Love Low-Maintenance Relationships

Let's talk upkeep…

Solar panels are the dream employees - they don't complain, they don't call in sick, and they don't need much supervision.

Once installed, they pretty much take care of themselves.

An occasional cleaning and a yearly inspection are all they ask for in return.

They have no moving parts, so there's nothing to wear out or break down.

If only your forklift fleet were this reliable.

6. Instant Savings on Electricity Bills

Big rooftops mean big electricity needs.

If you're running heavy machinery, lighting up a warehouse, or powering HVAC systems, you're probably spending a fortune on electricity.

Solar panels can offset a significant chunk of that cost - sometimes even eliminating it entirely.

Imagine looking at your electricity bill and seeing a big, fat zero where the total used to be. That's the kind of thing that makes CFOs cry tears of joy.

Contact me:

7. Cool Roof, Cooler Building

Here's a bonus you might not have considered…

Solar panels can help regulate the temperature of your building.

By covering your roof, they reduce heat absorption, keeping your facility cooler in the summer.

This means lower cooling costs and happier employees (unless you were using the heat to keep them awake).

Think of it as giving your building a hat - and not just any hat, but one that saves you money every time the sun shines.

8. Solar Panels Are Silent Workers

Unlike your machinery, which hums, clangs, and occasionally screeches, solar panels are silent.

They don't make noise, they don't disrupt operations, and they don't care if it's Monday morning. They just sit there quietly, generating energy.

It's like hiring a team of introverts who never need meetings or performance reviews.

9. The Green Factor: Instant Street Cred

Want to impress clients, partners, and eco-conscious customers?

Go solar.

Installing solar panels is like putting a giant neon sign on your building that says, "We care about the planet - and we're saving money while we're at it."

Today's consumers are increasingly choosing companies that prioritise sustainability.

By going solar, you're not just reducing your carbon footprint - you're boosting your brand.

And let's face it, everyone loves a company that's both smart and green.

10. Government Incentives: Free Money, Anyone?

Depending on your location, installing solar panels could make you eligible for some sweet government perks.

We're talking tax breaks, grants, and even payments for feeding excess energy back into the grid.

It's like the government saying, "Thanks for helping save the planet. Here's some extra cash for your trouble." And who doesn't love free money?

11. Futureproofing Your Business

Electricity prices are as unpredictable as the British weather.

One minute they're manageable, the next they're skyrocketing.

By investing in solar, you're locking in stable energy costs for the next 25 years or more.

Think of it as a hedge against inflation - except instead of gold, you're investing in sunlight. And unlike gold, sunlight doesn't run out or get stolen.

12. A Roof That Finally Pays for Itself

Your roof has been freeloading for years. It's time for it to pull its weight.

By installing solar panels, you're turning an expense into an asset. Suddenly, your roof isn't just an overhead - it's a profit centre.

And the best part?

Solar panels typically pay for themselves within a few years. After that, it's pure savings.

It's like buying a goose that lays golden eggs, except instead of eggs, it's kilowatts.

Conclusion: Put Your Roof to Work

Your sprawling, underutilised rooftop isn't just a roof - it's a business opportunity. Solar panels are the perfect way to unlock its potential, turning it into a money-saving, planet-saving powerhouse.

So, stop letting your roof laze around like a sunbathing teenager.

Give it a job, slap on some solar panels, and watch as it transforms into the hardest-working part of your building.

Because when it comes to saving money and going green, the sky really is the limit.

Chapter 4: 5 Signs You Have the Perfect Roof for Solar Panels

Congratulations! You Have a Roof

Let's start with the basics…

If your building has a roof, you're already halfway to joining the solar revolution. But not just any roof will do. Some rooftops are better suited for solar panels than others.

How can you tell if yours is one of them? Don't worry - we've got you covered.

Here are five surefire signs that your roof is ready to become a solar superstar:

1. Your Rooftop Seagulls Wear Sunglasses

If your local flock of rooftop seagulls squint and throw on their aviators as soon as the sun comes up, it's a dead giveaway: your roof gets plenty of sunlight.

Seagulls are practically nature's solar consultants - they know a sunny spot when they see one.

Solar panels thrive on direct sunlight, and if your roof is catching rays like a professional sunbather, you've got yourself a prime candidate for a solar installation.

Bonus points if your roof gets uninterrupted sunlight from morning until evening, because that's when solar panels work their magic.

Test It Yourself...

- Step 1: Go to the roof on a sunny day.
- Step 2: Stand there for 10 minutes.
- Step 3: If you start sweating profusely and questioning your life choices, congratulations!

Your roof gets excellent sunlight.

2. Your Roof Is So Flat, It Could Be a Pancake

Not to pick on sloped roofs, but flat roofs are the Beyoncé of the solar world—everybody loves them.

Why?

Because flat roofs offer maximum flexibility for panel installation.

It's like having a blank canvas to work with.

If your roof is flatter than a pancake, solar installers will love you. They can position the panels at the perfect angle to catch the most sunlight.

Even better, flat roofs make maintenance a breeze - no climbing at weird angles or risking your neck to clean a panel.

Warning Signs Your Roof May Be Too Sloped:

- Your roof doubles as a neighbourhood sledding hill in the winter.
- The thought of walking on your roof makes you dizzy.
- Any panel installed up there would double as a ski jump.

3. Your Roof Isn't Hosting the Local Rainforest

Let's get real…

Solar panels don't like shade. They thrive in direct sunlight, so if your roof is overshadowed by massive trees, nearby buildings, or an oversized inflatable Santa during the holidays, you might have a problem.

Signs your roof *might* be too shady:

- A family of squirrels has moved into the overhanging tree branches.
- You find moss up there more often than sunlight.
- Your solar installer shows up and immediately mutters, "Well, this is going to be a challenge."

The good news?

If your roof is mostly clear and free of obstruction, you're good to go. Just keep an eye on those pesky trees - they grow faster than you think.

4. Your Roof Could Host a Helicopter Landing

Size matters in the solar world.

The bigger your roof, the more panels you can install.

And the more panels you install, the more energy you can generate.

It's simple maths: big roof = big energy savings.

If your roof is so large that someone once joked about landing a helicopter on it, you've hit the solar jackpot.

Industrial buildings with sprawling rooftops are perfect for large-scale solar systems.

Think of your roof as the solar equivalent of an all-you-can-eat buffet: the bigger it is, the more energy it can devour.

Fun Size Comparisons:

- If your roof is the size of a football pitch, congratulations, you've got space for enough solar panels to power a small village.
- If it's closer to the size of a tennis court, don't worry - you can still generate significant energy.
- If your roof is smaller than your office desk - maybe stick to energy-saving light bulbs.

5. Your Roof Is Sturdier Than Your Monday Morning Coffee

Solar panels are lightweight compared to most industrial equipment, but they're not feather-light.

Your roof needs to be strong enough to support them for 20–30 years without throwing a tantrum (or, worse, collapsing).

Signs your roof is up for the challenge:

- It survived that one time you accidentally parked a forklift on it (don't ask).

Contact me:

- Your maintenance team has nicknamed it "The Fortress."
- It didn't flinch during last year's freak hailstorm.

If your roof is in good condition and structurally sound, you're ready to install panels.

If it's old, creaky, or looks like it's one gust of wind away from retirement, you might want to address that first.

Bonus Sign: Your Accountant Is Smiling at the Numbers

Okay, this one isn't about the roof itself, but it's still important.

If your electricity bills are high and your business has a sprawling, underutilised rooftop, solar panels can be a financial game-changer.

When your accountant crunches the numbers and starts smiling (instead of groaning), you know you're onto something.

Solar panels can save your business thousands of pounds annually, reduce your carbon footprint, and pay for themselves within a few years.

Plus, they come with financing options that make the transition easier than ever.

What If You Don't Have the Perfect Roof?

Even if your roof isn't ticking all these boxes, don't panic.

Solar installers are pros at making things work.

Sloped roof? They've got brackets for that.

A bit of shade? No problem - new technology can optimise panel performance even in less-than-ideal conditions.

Remember: perfection is great, but good enough can still save you a ton of money.

The Takeaway

If your rooftop is sunny, flat (or at least moderately sloped), clear of shade, spacious, and sturdy, you've got the solar equivalent of a prime beachfront property.

Solar panels will love living up there, and your wallet will love the energy savings.

And if your rooftop seagulls are already wearing sunglasses, well, that's just the universe telling you it's time to go solar.

Don't ignore the signs - your roof has been waiting for this moment.

Chapter 5: Electricity Bills: The Villain of Your Balance Sheet

Let's Start with the Elephant in the Room: Your Electricity Bill.

If your electricity bill is so high it should come with its own theme music, you're not alone.

Manufacturing and engineering companies are notorious for guzzling electricity like a teenager devouring pizza.

Between powering heavy machinery, running HVAC systems, and keeping the lights on in your cavernous facilities, you might feel like you're single-handedly funding your local utility company's annual holiday party.

But what if I told you there's a way to break free from the tyranny of high electricity costs?

A way to turn the tables on your utility company and start saving thousands every month? That's right - solar panels are here to flip the script.

1. Why Your Electricity Bill Feels Like a Punch in the Gut

Let's break it down…

As a manufacturing or engineering company, you rely on electricity to keep your operations running smoothly:

- Those CNC machines? Electricity hogs.
- Conveyor belts? More like money belts - draining cash as they run.
- Lighting up a warehouse the size of a football pitch? That's not free, either.
- And don't even get me started on air conditioning in the summer.

Every piece of equipment, every overhead light, every cup of coffee brewed in the breakroom is adding up. By the end of the month, your electricity bill might look less like a utility invoice and more like a ransom note.

2. How Solar Panels Flip the Script

Imagine this…

Instead of dreading your electricity bill, you look forward to it.

Sounds impossible, right? Not with solar. Here's the magic of solar panels:

1. **They Generate Free Electricity**: Once you've installed them, solar panels start producing electricity from sunlight - a resource that costs you absolutely nothing.

2. **They Reduce Your Reliance on the Grid**: The more energy you produce, the less you need to buy from the utility company. It's like cutting out the middleman and going straight to the source.

3. **They Pay for Themselves**: Over time, the savings on your electricity bill will cover the cost of your solar installation - and then some.

3. How Much Can Solar Save You?

Let's do some quick maths…

Say your business spends £10,000 a month on electricity.

A well-designed solar system could offset 50–70% of that cost, saving you £5,000–£7,000 every single month.

Over a year, that's £60,000–£84,000 in savings.

Over 25 years (the typical lifespan of solar panels), you're looking at £1.5 million or more in savings.

That's enough to:

- Buy a fleet of forklifts made of gold (not recommended).
- Give your employees raises and still have cash left over.

- Or, you know, just keep your CFO from having a meltdown every month.

4. Solar vs. Utility Rates: The Battle of the Century

Here's the thing about utility rates - they rarely go down.

In fact, they seem to rise faster than your blood pressure during quarterly reviews.

Solar panels, on the other hand, lock in your energy costs.

Once your system is paid off, your electricity is essentially free.

Let's compare:

- **Utility Company**: "Oh, you need power? That'll be £0.30 per kilowatt-hour this year. Next year? Who knows - maybe £0.35? We'll send you the bill!"
- **Solar Panels**: "We've got you covered for the next 25 years. No rate hikes, no surprises."

It's like choosing between an unpredictable landlord and a paid-off mortgage.

5. Cash Positive from Day One

You might be thinking...

"Sure, solar sounds great, but I don't have the cash to pay for it upfront."

No problem!

Solar financing options make it easy to go solar without breaking the bank.

Here's how:

1. **Asset Finance Solutions**:

Spread the cost of your solar system over several years while enjoying immediate savings on your electricity bill.

The monthly savings often outweigh the finance payments, meaning you're cash positive from day one.

2. **Power Purchase Agreements (PPAs) or Free to Fit**:

For businesses with large rooftops and high electricity spends, some providers will install solar panels for free and sell you the electricity at a lower rate than your utility company. You save money without spending a penny on installation.

6. The Environmental Bonus: Green is the New Gold

Let's not forget the PR benefits of going solar...

Today's clients and customers love companies that are eco-friendly.

By switching to solar, you're not just saving money - you're reducing your carbon footprint and showing the world that your business is serious about sustainability.

Imagine the marketing opportunities:

- "Powered by the Sun" signs on your building.
- A dedicated page on your website touting your green credentials.
- Awards from environmental groups for your commitment to renewable energy.

Suddenly, solar isn't just a financial decision - it's a branding goldmine.

7. What Can You Do with the Savings?

Let's say you've installed solar panels and are now saving thousands of pounds a month. What do you do with all that extra cash? Here are some ideas:

Contact me:

- **Upgrade Your Equipment**: New machines mean higher efficiency and more output.
- **Expand Your Operations**: Use the savings to fund new projects or hire more staff.
- **Throw a Party**: Celebrate your solar success with a company BBQ (powered by solar, of course).
- **Save for a Rainy Day**: Or, you know, reinvest the savings to future-proof your business.

8. Common Myths About Solar – Debunked

"But what about cloudy days?"

Solar panels still generate electricity even when it's cloudy - just not as much.

Think of it like working from home: productivity dips slightly, but things still get done.

"Aren't solar panels expensive?"

They used to be, but prices have dropped significantly in the last decade.

Plus, with financing options and government incentives, the upfront cost is manageable.

"Will they break if it hails?"

Modern solar panels are built to withstand extreme weather, including hailstorms.

If they can handle Mother Nature's mood swings, they can handle your rooftop.

9. The Bottom Line: Stop Renting Your Electricity

Think of your electricity bill as rent…

Every month, you're paying for something you'll never own.

Solar panels, on the other hand, are like buying a home.

Once they're paid off, the electricity they generate is yours to keep.

10. Ready to Ditch High Electricity Bills?

If you're tired of watching your profits evaporate into your utility company's bank account, it's time to make the switch.

Solar panels are a game-changer for manufacturing and engineering companies.

They're reliable, cost-effective, and - best of all - they'll turn your biggest expense into one of your smartest investments.

Contact me:

So, why not let the sun do some of the heavy lifting?

It's been shining for billions of years, and it's not planning to stop anytime soon.

Chapter 6: Solar ROI, Asset Finance, and Free-to-Fit: Saving Money (and the Planet) One Slice at a Time

Let's Talk About Return on Investment: Solar's Secret Sauce.

When most business owners hear the words "solar panels," they think one thing: *expensive*.

But what if I told you that solar isn't just an expense - it's an investment?

And not just any investment - a fast, reliable, money-saving superhero dressed in photovoltaic cells.

Stick with me, and I'll explain how paying for solar is less like buying a car and more like buying a pizza oven that pumps out cash instead of pepperoni pies.

Part 1: The Fast Return on Investment or, Solar Panels Make Money Faster Than You Can Burn It

Imagine this scenario…

You fork out £100,000 to install solar panels on your factory's roof.

That's a big chunk of cash, right?

But here's the kicker - those panels immediately start saving you £5,000 a month on electricity bills.

Let's do the math (I promise it's the fun kind):

- **£5,000 a month in savings** = £60,000 per year.
- **Payback time?** A little over **1.5 years**.

By the second year, the panels have paid for themselves, and every pound you save after that goes straight into your pocket.

It's like planting a money tree - except instead of water, all it needs is sunlight (and no one has to call HR when it grows through the roof).

Solar ROI in Context:

Paying for solar upfront is like buying a pizza oven for your pizzeria.

Sure, it's expensive at first, but after a year of pumping out perfectly crispy crusts, that ovens paid for itself - and now it's pure profit.

Except solar doesn't burn dough. It saves it.

Part 2: Asset Finance – Like a Pizza Delivery Service for Solar

Now, not everyone has cash lying around to pay for solar panels upfront.

Maybe you've got payroll to meet, machines to upgrade, or, let's be honest, a coffee machine in the breakroom that needs replacing *again*.

That's where **asset finance** comes in - a way to go solar without raiding the company safe.

How Asset Finance Works (The Pizza Delivery Metaphor Edition):

Think of it like ordering pizza from your favourite takeaway joint:

1. You're hungry (or in this case, sick of your electricity bills).

2. You order the pizza (a.k.a. the solar panels).

3. The delivery driver shows up, you get to eat (the panels start generating electricity), but here's the best part:

4. **You pay later.**

With asset finance, your solar system gets installed right away, and you make monthly payments over time.

But here's the kicker: the **money you save on electricity** each month is often **more than the monthly finance payment.**

Example:

- **Monthly Electricity Bill (Before Solar):** £10,000.
- **Monthly Finance Payment:** £5,000.
- **New Monthly Electricity Bill (With Solar):** £2,000.
- **Net Savings:** £3,000/month.

This is why asset finance can be considered **cash-positive** from day one.

You're literally saving money while paying for your panels.

It's like ordering a pizza and finding out the delivery driver also paid your rent that month.

Part 3: Free-to-Fit Solar Solutions – XXL Roofs, King-Sized Savings

Now, let's say your business has an **XXL rooftop** - we're talking sprawling, football-field-sized expanses that are currently home to nothing but pigeons and the occasional stray frisbee.

And let's say your electricity bills are similarly king-sized, hitting five or even six figures every month.

In this case, there's a magical option called **free-to-fit solar** (a.k.a. the "Power Purchase Agreement" or PPA).

What Is Free-to-Fit Solar?

Let's stick with the pizza analogy. Imagine this:

- A fancy pizza restaurant offers to build you a **free pizza oven**.
- They'll handle the installation, maintenance, and upkeep.
- In return, you agree to buy their pizza for the next 25 years at a **discounted rate** compared to what you were paying before.

That's how a PPA works.

A solar company installs the panels at no cost to you. In return, you agree to buy the electricity they produce at a lower rate than your current utility bill.

The XXL Rooftop Example:

- Your current electricity bill is £50,000/month.
- The solar company installs a free-to-fit system that powers 70% of your facility.
- Now, you're paying £25,000 to the solar company and £10,000 to the grid.
- **Net Savings:** £15,000/month.

You save money **without spending a single penny upfront.** It's like getting free pizza *and* losing weight.

Part 4: Why These Options Work for Manufacturing and Engineering Companies

Manufacturing and engineering companies are the perfect candidates for these solar solutions because:

1. **Big Roofs, Big Potential**: Your facilities often have enormous rooftops, which are perfect for large-scale solar installations.

2. **High Energy Usage**: The more electricity you use, the more you save by going solar.

3. **Long-Term Thinking**: Your business plans span decades, just like solar panels, which have a lifespan of 25+ years.

Part 5: The Humorous Benefits of Going Solar

Still not convinced?

Here's how solar will make your life better (and funnier):

1. **Your Accountant Will Cry Tears of Joy**:

Instead of panic attacks every time the electricity bill arrives, your accountant can finally relax - and maybe even crack a smile.

2. **No More Surprise Rate Hikes**:

Utility companies are like weather in the UK - unpredictable and occasionally infuriating. Solar locks in your rates, so you know exactly what to expect.

3. **Your Rooftop Becomes a Tourist Attraction**:

Okay, maybe not officially, but employees will love showing off the company's shiny new solar panels. Bonus points if the seagulls start hosting rooftop raves.

4. **You'll Be the Office Hero**:

Saving money *and* saving the planet? You'll go down in company history as the boss who made it happen.

Part 6: Let the Sun Work for You

In summary, whether you're paying cash for a fast ROI, opting for cash-positive asset finance, or taking advantage of free-to-fit solar, there's an option that works for your business.

And the best part? You'll start saving money immediately.

So, what are you waiting for?

The sun's been doing its job for 4.6 billion years - it's time to let it do some heavy lifting for your electricity bill, too.

And who knows? Maybe someday your rooftop seagulls will send you a thank-you card.

Contact me:

Chapter 7: Solar Myths Busted: The Truth About Panels, Roofs, and the Weather

Ah, solar panels. Magical rectangles that turn sunlight into electricity, save money, and help the environment.

But let's be honest - there are plenty of myths and misconceptions swirling around solar energy.

From "Will they work in the rain?" to "Are they secretly alien technology?" (spoiler alert: they're not), it's time to separate fact from fiction.

So, grab a cup of coffee, and let's shine some light on these myths - with a healthy dose of humour.

1. "Do They Work in the Rain? Or Are Solar Panels Fair-Weather Friends?"

Let's start with the most common misconception…

"Solar panels only work on sunny days." It's understandable. After all, they're called *solar* panels, not *rainbow* panels.

But here's the truth…

Solar panels still work in the rain, on cloudy days, and even during a good old-fashioned British drizzle.

Why?

Solar panels generate electricity from light, not heat.

As long as there's daylight (even filtered through clouds), your panels will be working.

Sure, they're not as efficient during a thunderstorm as they are on a sunny day, but they don't just take the day off because it's a bit gloomy.

Real-World Analogy…

Think of solar panels as a solar-powered mood ring:

- On sunny days, they're glowing with productivity.
- On cloudy days, they're still working, just not as enthusiastically.
- On pitch-black nights? Okay, you caught them - they're off-duty. But that's why we have batteries and the grid to keep things running.

Fun Fact:

Some studies suggest that **cooler, rainy days can actually help improve solar efficiency** because panels perform better when they're not overheated.

So, while the rain might dampen your outdoor plans, it won't stop your solar panels from doing their job.

2. "Will Solar Panels Damage My Roof? Or Is My Roof About to Star in a Disaster Movie?"

Next up…

"Will solar panels destroy my roof?"

It's a valid concern. After all, your roof is the unsung hero of your building - keeping you dry, warm, and safe from falling meteorites (hopefully).

The good news?

Solar panels won't damage your roof - if anything, they'll help protect it.

How?

- **Shield from the Elements**: Solar panels act like a second layer of armour for your roof, shielding it from

rain, hail, and even those pesky UV rays that can wear down shingles over time.
- **Proper Installation**: Professional installers don't just slap panels onto your roof with duct tape and hope for the best. They use specialised mounting systems designed to keep your roof intact and watertight.

Myth-Busting Q&A:

Q: What about holes in the roof from the mounts?

A: Don't worry - installers use sealants and flashing to make sure everything is secure and waterproof. Your roof won't spring leaks just because you went solar.

Q: What if my roof isn't in great shape?

A: If your roof is older than your company's founding date, you might want to replace it before going solar. Think of it as giving your roof a glow-up to match the sleek new panels.

Bonus: Solar Panels Can Extend Your Roof's Life

By protecting your roof from direct sunlight and harsh weather, solar panels can actually help it last longer.

It's like putting sunglasses on your roof - it looks cooler and ages more gracefully.

3. "Are Solar Panels Secretly Alien Technology?"

Ah, the age-old conspiracy theory…

"Solar panels are too advanced. They must be from another world!"

Let's debunk this one once and for all.

Spoiler Alert: Solar Panels Are 100% Earth-Made

The science behind solar panels is impressive, sure, but it's not alien.

Here's how they work:

- Sunlight hits the solar cells, which are made of silicon (a material you can find right here on Earth).
- The cells generate an electric current, which is then converted into usable electricity.
- You use that electricity to power your lights, machines, and, let's be honest, the office coffee machine.

Why Do People Think They're Alien?

1. **They Seem Futuristic**: Turning sunlight into electricity feels like something out of a sci-fi movie. But remember, humans also invented the internet, which is arguably weirder.

2. **They're Silent**: Unlike noisy generators, solar panels just sit there quietly, doing their job. No whirring, no buzzing—just clean energy.

If solar panels were alien technology, don't you think they'd come with cooler features? Like a built-in Wi-Fi hotspot or a laser show?

4. Other Hilarious Misconceptions About Solar Panels

"Do Solar Panels Make My Roof Hotter?"

Nope.

In fact, they can help keep your building cooler by absorbing sunlight that would otherwise heat up your roof.

It's like giving your building a giant pair of sunglasses and an SPF 50 hat.

"Will Birds Build Nests Under My Panels?"

Okay, this one's not entirely a myth - birds do love a good hiding spot.

But most installers use mesh or barriers to prevent feathered freeloaders from moving in.

Your roof won't turn into a pigeon palace.

"Do Solar Panels Stop Working After 10 Years?"

Absolutely not.

Most panels are designed to last 25–30 years, and they still generate electricity even after that - just at slightly reduced efficiency.

Think of them like a reliable old car: not as fast as they used to be, but still getting the job done.

5. The Bottom Line: Why Solar Myths Are No Match for Facts

Solar panels aren't magic, alien technology, or roof-destroying terrors.

They're a practical, efficient, and environmentally friendly way to save money and reduce your carbon footprint.

Contact me:

And while they might not work at night (yet - get on it, science!), they're more than capable of powering your business during the day, rain or shine.

So, the next time someone tells you that solar panels won't work because "it's too cloudy" or "they'll break my roof," feel free to hit them with the truth - and maybe a bit of humour, too.

And if they still insist on believing that solar panels are alien tech, well, let's just say that's one conspiracy we're happy to be a part of. Who wouldn't want to harness the power of the sun, alien-approved or not?

Chapter 8: Going Solar: The Ultimate Green Glow-Up for Your Business

When you think about solar panels, you probably picture energy savings, sustainability, and that warm fuzzy feeling of doing something good for the planet.

But here's something you might not have considered: **solar panels are also a PR powerhouse.**

In today's eco-conscious world, nothing screams "We care about the planet" like a rooftop full of glittering solar panels.

And for businesses looking to attract green-minded clients, going solar isn't just a smart move - it's practically a VIP pass to the sustainability club.

Let's dive into how going solar can boost your green credentials and leave your clients impressed.

1. Green Credentials: The Shiny Badge of Honor

Let's face it: everyone loves a good "green" story.

Whether it's companies pledging to go carbon-neutral or influencers posting about reusable water bottles, sustainability is the new cool.

And by going solar, your business gets to wear the ultimate eco-friendly badge of honour.

Imagine this...

- You've got rows of solar panels sparkling on your roof.
- You casually mention in meetings, "Oh yes, we generate 70% of our electricity on-site."
- Clients look at you like you've just announced free coffee and biscuits for life.

Going solar doesn't just make you environmentally responsible - it makes you *look* environmentally responsible. And perception matters.

Fun Fact:

Research shows that **75% of consumers prefer to do business with environmentally friendly companies.**

Translation?

Your solar panels aren't just saving the planet; they're also winning you clients.

Contact me:

2. First Impressions Matter: Solar Panels as the Ultimate Welcome Mat

Picture this…

A potential client pulls up to your facility. They step out of their car and look up to see your rooftop glittering with solar panels. What's their first thought?

- "Wow, this company cares about sustainability."
- "They must be forward-thinking and innovative."
- "I should have brought sunglasses; this is blindingly impressive."

That's the kind of first impression solar panels create.

They tell the world, "We're not just in it for profit—we're in it for progress."

And let's be honest, who wouldn't want to do business with a company that's literally *powered by the sun*?

3. Eco-Conscious Clients: The Green Seal of Approval

If your clients care about sustainability - and let's be real, most do these days - going solar is like rolling out a green carpet for them.

Here's How It Works...

1. **Clients See Your Solar Panels**

"Wow, they're serious about reducing their carbon footprint!"

2. **Clients Feel Good About Doing Business with You**

"Partnering with this company aligns with our own sustainability goals!"

3. **Clients Tell Everyone About You**

"We work with a solar-powered company. We're basically saving the planet together."

Case Study: The "Eco Hero" Effect

Imagine your client is a manufacturer that also values sustainability.

When they choose to work with you, they're not just getting your products or services - they're also associating themselves with your green credentials.

It's a win-win: you get their business, and they get to brag about partnering with an eco-friendly supplier.

4. Solar Panels as the Ultimate Conversation Starter

Solar panels aren't just functional - they're a statement. And statements spark conversations.

Client Tour Scenario:

Client: "Are those solar panels on your roof?"

You (grinning): "Yes, they are. We generate most of our electricity right here. It's all part of our commitment to sustainability."

Client: "That's amazing! Tell me more."

You: *slides into a humble brag about your carbon savings and reduced energy costs*

By the end of the tour, your client is already sold - not just on your product, but on your values.

5. The Marketing Goldmine of Going Solar

Solar panels aren't just an energy solution - they're a marketing tool.

Think about it:

- Press releases announcing your new solar system.
- Social media posts showing off your panels.

- A "Green Commitment" page on your website.

Every time you talk about your solar panels, you're reinforcing your brand as an eco-friendly, forward-thinking business.

It's like giving your marketing team a shiny new toy to play with - except this toy also saves you money on electricity.

The Instagram Effect

Solar panels might not be as cute as cats or as glamorous as food photos, but they *are* photogenic.

A well-lit shot of your solar-powered facility is perfect for your next LinkedIn or Instagram post.

Bonus points if you can catch the panels glistening at sunrise or reflecting a dramatic sky.

6. Nothing Says, "We Care About the Planet" Like Glittering Panels

Solar panels are the modern-day equivalent of a knight's shining armour - except instead of fighting dragons, they're battling carbon emissions.

They're a visual declaration that your company cares about the planet, sustainability, and the future.

And let's be real: glittering panels just look cool. They give your rooftop an air of sophistication, like your building is wearing designer sunglasses.

7. Why Solar Is a Must-Have for Modern Businesses

In a world where climate change is everyone's business, going solar isn't just an option—it's a necessity.

Here's why:

1. Clients Demand It

Eco-conscious clients want to work with companies that share their values. Going solar tells them, "We care about the same things you do."

2. Employees Love It

Millennials and Gen Z workers are passionate about sustainability. A solar-powered workplace makes them proud to work for you.

3. It Future-Proofs Your Business

As more companies commit to carbon reduction goals, being ahead of the curve gives you a competitive edge.

8. Closing Thoughts: Solar Panels Are the Ultimate Flex

At the end of the day, going solar is about more than just saving money (though that's a big perk).

It's about making a statement—to your clients, your employees, and the world.

When clients see those glittering panels on your roof, they'll know you're not just another business.

You're a leader, an innovator, and a company that genuinely cares about the planet.

So go ahead, install those panels, and let them shine.

Because nothing says "We've got our act together" like a solar-powered building - and nothing says "We care about the planet" like glittering panels catching the morning sun.

Chapter 9: Smiling CFOs and Sunny Profits: How Energy Savings Brighten the Bottom Line

If there's one universal truth in the business world, it's this: CFOs don't smile easily.

For many, it takes a miracle - or at least a fiscal quarter with zero unexpected expenses.

Yet, there's one thing guaranteed to turn even the most stoic finance chief into a grinning optimist: **solar energy savings.**

Yes, you heard that right…

Solar panels don't just save the planet; they save your bottom line.

And when your energy bills shrink faster than a wool sweater in the dryer, even the grumpiest CFOs can't help but crack a smile.

Let's dive into how solar slashes costs and boosts profitability - with a few anecdotes of CFOs who finally found something to grin about.

1. The Energy Bill Epiphany: "Wait, this is real?"

The first step to CFO happiness begins with the monthly electricity bill.

Before solar, it's a dreaded envelope (or email notification) that's opened with the care of a bomb disposal expert.

But after solar?

That bill shrinks faster than a company retreat budget during a downturn.

Anecdote: The Day the CFO Smiled

Take Lisa, CFO of a midsize manufacturing company.

Her team installed solar panels last year, but she remained sceptical. "Let's see if this so-called 'savings' shows up on paper," she muttered.

The first month post-installation, she opened the electricity bill - and gasped.

It was 60% lower.

She stared at the numbers, her usual furrowed brow lifting into… was that a grin? Her assistant, shocked, whispered, "Lisa, you're… smiling?"

"I just realised," Lisa said, eyes twinkling, "I might actually approve this year's Christmas party budget."

Contact me:

2. ROI: Faster Than Your Favourite Delivery Service

One of the biggest advantages of going solar is the **fast return on investment (ROI).**

For companies paying cash, the payback period can be as short as 2 - 4 years.

That's like investing in a startup and actually seeing profits before your next birthday.

Fun Fact:

The moment a CFO hears "ROI in under four years," they experience a fleeting moment of pure joy, like spotting a tax deduction they didn't know existed.

3. Profitability 101: Fewer Expenses = Bigger Smiles

Energy savings go straight to your bottom line.

Every pound saved on electricity is a pound that stays in your business.

This simple equation delights CFOs no end.

Anecdote: From Grumpy to Giddy

James, the CFO of a regional engineering firm, was notorious for his grim demeanour.

His team joked that his favorite word was "No."

No to new software, no to team lunches, and definitely no to anything labeled "green initiative."

But when the company installed solar panels, James couldn't argue with the numbers. Within three months, energy costs had dropped by £5,000 per month.

At the next staff meeting, James walked in with pastries. Someone whispered, "Who is this man, and what did he do with James?"

4. The Secret Sauce: Predictable Energy Costs

Solar isn't just about saving money - it's about controlling costs.

When you generate your own power, you're no longer at the mercy of fluctuating energy prices.

This predictability makes CFOs giddy because it allows for accurate budgeting.

Fun Analogy:

Imagine your energy bill is usually like an unpredictable rollercoaster. Solar turns it into the kiddie ride: smooth, steady, and completely under control.

5. CFOs Love Assets That Pay for Themselves

Solar panels are the gift that keeps on giving.

Once installed, they generate free electricity for decades, effectively paying for themselves over time.

And for CFOs, there's nothing better than an asset that pulls its weight.

Anecdote: The Smug CFO

Susan, CFO of a distribution company, loved bragging about her "smart investments." After going solar, she had a new favourite story.

"See that roof?" she'd say, pointing at the glittering panels during client visits. "That's not just a roof; that's a money machine. And it doesn't take lunch breaks."

6. The Ripple Effect: Solar Savings Enable Smart Spending

When energy bills plummet, companies suddenly find themselves with extra cash. CFOs use this newfound wiggle room to invest in growth initiatives, upgrade equipment, or finally fix that coffee machine in the break room.

Anecdote: The Budget Transformation

Before solar, Tom, the CFO of a packaging company, was constantly battling budget constraints. "We can't afford it" was practically his motto.

But post-solar, Tom discovered they were saving £8,000 a month on electricity.

Suddenly, he was approving marketing campaigns, new forklifts, and even a shiny new office plant. His team started calling him "Santa Tom."

7. Tax Breaks: The Cherry on Top

Governments love renewable energy, which means generous tax incentives for businesses that go solar.

These rebates and credits are like the icing on the cake - or as CFOs call them, "free money."

Anecdote: The Tax Credit Revelation

When Mia, CFO of a food processing company, realised the solar investment came with a hefty tax credit, she nearly fell out of her chair. "You mean we get to save money *and* reduce our taxes? Why didn't anyone tell me this before?"

Her team replied, "We did, but you were too busy calculating depreciation schedules."

8. The PR Perks: More Clients, More Smiles

Going solar doesn't just save money - it attracts eco-conscious clients.

And more clients mean more revenue, which leads to the ultimate CFO fantasy: exceeding quarterly projections.

Anecdote: The Solar Sell

After installing solar panels, a construction firm landed a major contract with a sustainability-focused retailer.

The retailer chose them specifically because of their green initiatives.

When the deal closed, their CFO stood up, clapped his hands, and said, "Well, that's the easiest ROI I've ever approved."

9. The Legacy Factor: CFOs and the Long Game

CFOs love thinking long-term, and solar panels are the epitome of a forward-thinking investment.

With a lifespan of 25–30 years, they provide value long after the initial payback period.

Anecdote: The Legacy Builder

Emma, CFO of a logistics company, saw solar as her chance to leave a mark.

"In 20 years, when I'm sipping cocktails on a beach, this company will still be saving money because of my decision. You're welcome, future CFOs."

10. The Final Smile: Solar = Happiness

At the end of the day, solar panels don't just change your energy bills - they change the way CFOs see the world.

They turn sceptics into believers, penny-pinchers into spenders, and frowns into grins.

So, if your CFO hasn't smiled in years, maybe it's time to suggest solar. After all, nothing brightens a bottom line - or a boardroom - like a little sunshine.

Chapter 10: "Solar Power - No, It Won't Fry Your Toaster"

Solar panels have become the rock stars of renewable energy, strutting their shiny surfaces across rooftops and fields worldwide.

But they also come with their fair share of questions - some practical, some… well, let's say "creative."

Whether you're a business owner wondering if they'll save you cash or a curious customer asking if they'll power your espresso machine on a cloudy day, we've got you covered.

1. Do solar panels work when it's cloudy?

Yes, they do!

Clouds may reduce the panels' efficiency, but they won't leave you in the dark.

Think of solar panels as the overachievers in class: even when it's gloomy, they'll do their homework - just not as quickly.

Weird Client Question:

"If I shine a flashlight on the panels during a blackout, will that generate power?"

Only if you've got a flashlight powered by a star. Otherwise, no.

2. Will solar panels save my company money?

Absolutely.

But here's the catch - it's not instant.

Installing solar panels is like buying a lifetime supply of coffee beans instead of hitting Starbucks every morning.

Upfront, it's pricey, but over time, your wallet will thank you.

Bonus Tip: Check for local incentives and rebates. It's like finding out your coffee subscription comes with free cookies.

Weird Client Question:

"Can I use the savings to buy a jet ski?"

Sure, but maybe save up for the panels first.

3. How long do they last?

Solar panels usually last 25–30 years.

That's longer than most smartphones, laptops, and, dare I say, some business partnerships.

Fun Fact: They don't just "die" after 30 years.

They'll still work, but they might need some downtime - kind of like a retiree who occasionally babysits the grandkids.

Weird Client Question:

"Can I take my solar panels with me if I move?"

Technically, yes.

But it's like moving a grand piano - it's possible, but do you really want to?

4. Do I need a battery?

Not necessarily.

If you're connected to the grid, you can feed extra energy back and "borrow" it later.

Contact me:

A battery is handy for backup power, but it's not essential unless you're living off-grid or preparing for the zombie apocalypse.

Weird Client Question:

"Can I store solar energy in my old car batteries?"

Only if you want your car to explode in a dramatic, yet unproductive way.

5. What happens during a power outage?

If you don't have a battery or a specific type of inverter, your solar panels won't work during an outage.

Why?

Safety reasons. They don't want to accidentally zap the people fixing the grid.

Weird Client Question:

"Can I install a manual override and keep it secret?"

This isn't Mission Impossible. Please don't.

6. How much space do I need?

Solar panels don't take up much space - unless you're planning to power an entire amusement park.

A typical commercial building has plenty of roof space for a good setup.

Weird Client Question:

"Can I install panels on my RV's roof to power my hot tub?"

This is the kind of energy we love (pun intended).

Yes, but you might have to choose between heating the hot tub and cooking dinner.

7. Do they need a lot of maintenance?

Not really.

They're low maintenance, like succulents, but without the risk of overwatering.

Just keep them clean and free from debris.

If a bird claims your panels as their bathroom, give them a wash.

Weird Client Question:

"Can I install self-cleaning solar panels like self-cleaning ovens?"

Not yet, but when we do, they'll be life changing.

8. Are solar panels environmentally friendly?

Yes!

They're the Beyoncé of renewable energy - clean, efficient, and fabulous.

Producing them does have some environmental impact, but it's outweighed by the years of clean energy they provide.

Weird Client Question:

"Do solar panels attract aliens?"

Not unless your panels are shaped like a welcome mat and say, "We Come in Peace."

9. Can solar panels power everything?

Yes, with enough panels, you could power your entire business - or even a small village.

But realistically, you'll want to balance expectations with roof space, budget, and energy needs.

Weird Client Question:

"Can I use solar panels to charge my pet robot?"

Absolutely. And if it starts dancing under the panels, please record it.

10. What happens at night?

At night, your panels take a well-deserved nap.

If you've got a battery, it'll kick in.

Otherwise, you'll rely on grid power, which is perfectly fine.

Weird Client Question:

"Can I use moonlight to generate power?"

Technically, moonlight is just reflected sunlight, but it's too dim to do much.

So no, werewolf-friendly panels are not a thing.

Closing Remarks

Solar panels are an investment, but they're also a step into a cleaner, greener future.

Whether you're powering a factory or a fridge, they'll work tirelessly for you.

And yes, they can even charge your pet robot (or at least we hope so).

Final Weird Client Question:

"Can I paint my panels to match my brand colours?"

Only if you want them to stop working.

Panels like to soak up sunlight, not compliments.

Chapter 11: "The Sunny Side of Saving - A Conclusion That's Worth Its Weight in Watts"

Congratulations! You've made it to the end of our solar journey.

Hopefully, you've learned a lot about solar panels and only slightly questioned humanity after reading some of those "weird client questions."

Now, let's tie it all together with one big bow of sunlight.

This conclusion isn't just a farewell; it's a call to action—for your wallet, the planet, and your sanity.

1. Saving Money: The Bright Side of the Bottom Line

Let's start with the universal truth: Companies like money.

And solar panels? They're like the gift that keeps on giving.

Once you install them, your roof basically becomes an employee who never calls in sick, never asks for a raise, and works weekends for free.

Energy Savings:

Imagine reducing your electricity bills by 50%, 60%, or even more.

Over 25 years, that's enough to buy a small island - or at least a yacht to visit someone else's island.

Tax Incentives:

Governments love when companies go green, so they'll throw rebates and tax credits your way. Think of it as a "thank you" note from the planet, but in cash.

Humorous Tip:

Think of solar panels as your new corporate mascot.

Name them "Sunny McSavings" and throw them a birthday party each year for how much they've saved you.

2. Saving the Planet: The World Needs Heroes (and Solar Panels)

We know - it's tough to care about the ozone layer when you're focused on meeting quarterly goals.

Contact me:

But let's face it: the planet is your ultimate stakeholder. Solar panels aren't just about reducing costs; they're about reducing carbon footprints.

Cleaner Energy:

Solar power is 100% renewable.

The sun isn't going anywhere (well, not for another 5 billion years), so why not put it to work?

Corporate Responsibility:

Customers and clients increasingly value companies that prioritise sustainability.

A rooftop full of solar panels isn't just good PR; it's a badge of honour.

Humorous Tip:

If your competitors ask why your roof looks so futuristic, tell them you're building a space station. Let them stew while you save the planet.

3. Saving Yourself: Fewer Headaches, More Peace of Mind

Running a manufacturing or engineering company comes with enough challenges. Rising energy costs don't have to be one of them.

Solar panels take one of your largest variable costs and turn it into a fixed, predictable investment.

Energy Independence:

Say goodbye to the stress of fluctuating energy prices. With solar, you control your power destiny.

Low Maintenance:

Solar panels are the chillest part of your operation. A little cleaning, maybe a quick inspection, and they're good to go.

Humorous Tip:

Your panels will probably require less attention than your office coffee machine - and they'll never break down right before a big meeting.

4. Why Manufacturing and Engineering Companies Should Care

You already have the perfect setup: **a big, empty roof.**

Instead of letting it bake in the sun like an underappreciated parking lot, why not turn it into a money-saving power plant?

High Energy Needs:

Manufacturing and engineering operations use a lot of electricity. Solar panels can offset those costs in a big way.

Boosting the ROI of Unused Space:

Think of your roof as a blank canvas. Solar panels turn it into a masterpiece of efficiency, cost savings, and environmental stewardship.

Humorous Tip:

Your rooftop is basically freeloading. Put it to work and make it earn its keep.

5. Call to Action: Don't Wait for the Next Energy Price Hike - Go Solar Today!

Energy prices aren't going down. The time to act is now.

Every month you wait is another month of overpaying for electricity.

It's like watching money fly out the window - except the window is actually a power line.

Why Now?

- **Incentives won't last forever.** Governments have limited budgets for rebates and tax breaks, so it's a use-it-or-lose-it situation.
- **Energy costs are unpredictable.** Solar panels lock in your savings for decades.
- **Your competition isn't waiting.** Beat them to the sustainability punch and become a leader in your industry.

What's Next?

- **Step 1:** Contact a reputable solar provider for a consultation.
- **Step 2:** Get a custom plan tailored to your energy needs and roof space.

- **Step 3:** Watch your energy bills shrink while your reputation grows.

Final Thought: The Sun is Your Friend

Let's wrap this up with a bit of inspiration:

The sun shines every day, asking nothing in return. It doesn't charge a subscription fee, doesn't nag you for reviews, and never takes a holiday. It's time to let the sun power your business. Stop letting your roof just sit there, soaking up heat and offering zero value. Instead, transform it into a high-tech hub of energy savings and sustainability. Don't just think about it. Act on it.

"Go solar today - the only thing you have to lose is your electric bill!"

Chapter 12: About the Author

Darren Turner is a man with one foot in the business world and the other firmly planted on his solar panels.

As the author of 'Watts Up With Solar', Darren has taken his knack for turning complex industry jargon into digestible, laugh-out-loud wisdom to new heights—preferably on a roof where the sun can hit it.

Married to the ever-patient Nyreen, Darren is the proud (and often outsmarted) father of Samuel, Benjamin, and Scarlett.

Each child offers a unique take on whether Darren's solar obsession is "awesome" or "super embarrassing."

Darren's journey to renewable energy stardom began with a near-death experience - not from anything dramatic like a rogue solar panel falling from a roof - but from the soul-crushing pressures of running a failing business.

He turned that experience into his debut book, 'How a Greek Goddess Saved Our Business'.

Spoiler: it wasn't about mythology but rather a heroic pivot from product sales to a game-changing subscription service. (Though he did briefly consider naming his company after Athena.)

Contact me:

Over the years, Darren has operated an eco-friendly empire. From EV charging stations to solar panel solutions, his mission is clear: saving the planet whilst ensuring his neighbours never win at the power bill bragging game.

When he's not revolutionising carbon reduction, Darren starts and ends his days walking Shadow, his springer spaniel and unofficial business consultant.

With AirPods in and business books playing, he absorbs entrepreneurial advice while Shadow absorbs every muddy puddle.

In Darren's world, the future is bright—and, more importantly, solar-powered.

Whether he's on a rooftop, in a boardroom, or chasing Shadow through the park, you can bet he's dreaming up the next big eco-friendly idea. Or figuring out how to get mud off his shoes.

Contact me: